TO
....

From
....

Date
....

Note

Tips To Bring Your Coloring To The Next Level
First of all, pick coloring tools:

You can use pens, markers, pencils, or crayons. Choose whatever you

like in terms of texture and feeling. If I would do recommend, here it is.

I'd go with pencils for beginner. If you are wanting to play with some advanced

techniques or detail work, then go with a set of pencils and a set of markers.

Then of course you can throw in pens, crayons, lead pencils, and more later.

Palette/Theme or Better to pick a concept:

Picking color palettes is not easy. I used to spend more than an hours to see

professional talk about this. Thus, I recommend making it easier on yourself by using

available color palette online. You may search it very easy from Pinterest or

use design-seeds website. You will get much more idea to make your artwork

great and special.

Finally:

Just do it and let loose. Coloring is an effective stress management and

meditation. Let coloring be your calm and have a great

<u>Note</u>

<u>Note</u>

<u>Note</u>

<u>Note</u>

<u>Note</u>

Note

Note
Note

<u>**Note**</u>

<u>Note</u>

COFFEE
SWEET
NOTES

<u>Note</u>

<u>Note</u>

EYESHADOW
COFFEE

<u>Note</u>

<u>**Note**</u>

Note

<u>**Note**</u>

Follow
your
passion

<u>**Note**</u>

SWEET
NOTES
COFFEE

<u>**Note**</u>

SWEET
NOTES

<u>Note</u>

i love you
COFFEE

<u>Note</u>

COFFEE
SWEET
NOTES

<u>**Note**</u>

SWEET
NOTES
COFFEE

<u>**Note**</u>

<u>Note</u>

<u>Note</u>

<u>**Note**</u>

<u>Note</u>

9 781974 283361